NATIONAL BUS COMPANY

1972–86

Michael Hitchen

AMBERLEY

First published 2025

Amberley Publishing
The Hill, Stroud
Gloucestershire, GL5 4EP

www.amberley-books.com

Copyright © Michael Hitchen, 2025

The right of Michael Hitchen to be identified
as the Author of this work has been asserted
in accordance with the Copyright, Designs and
Patents Act 1988.

ISBN 978 1 3981 1885 0 (print)
ISBN 978 1 3981 1886 7 (ebook)

British Library Cataloguing in Publication Data.
A catalogue record for this book is available from
the British Library.

Origination by Amberley Publishing.
Printed in the UK.

Introduction

In 1972 the recently formed National Bus Company confidently pronounced 'Together we're really going places', though the publicly owned organisation had been formed a little earlier in 1969. It was the introduction of a corporate livery that really showed that the NBC had arrived. Fred Wood had been appointed as chairman in 1972, and his vision prompted the development of a corporate identity. Wood commissioned Norman Wilson and his business Norman Wilson Associates to design all aspects of our National bus image. This new, modern, corporate image would simplify liveries, helping the public identify with its ownership of the nation's bus services. In 1972 the first vehicles were presented to the NBC board outside a motel in the East Midlands – white for coaches, though initially yellow was considered, and with red or green for service buses. The dual purpose or local coach livery was not decided when instruction on buses were issued in early 1972, so some local interpretations were applied. After some minor experiments and oddments, such as cream corporate lettering on old liveries or the allowance of an NBC blue for a handful of companies, the livery was set from this early date, with only a minor change to the double N symbol by introducing red, white and blue colours. Things would remain static until the early 1980s when the NBC headquarters relaxed its tight guidance with the introduction of the 'Venetian blind' dual-purpose livery and allowance for constituent companies to develop localised liveries.

Between 1972 and 1986 the roads of England and Wales were served by the state-owned National Bus Company, carrying the corporate livery introduced, bringing the thirty-six or so bus and coach companies together. At the time with a fleet of over 20,000 vehicles, it was the largest bus company in the world. Being formed from individual companies, much individuality existed in its vehicle fleets. This, along with changes to operating areas and fleet amalgamations, made its short seventeen-year existence full of interests to the transport enthusiast. The make up of BET, BTC and a handful of independents made for huge amounts of variety underneath the poppy red, leaf green (not forgetting blue or yellow) and white paint. Many older vehicles would receive full corporate livery, alongside which the state-built Leyland National would be introduced to the majority of operators, giving a new generation of bus to the public. At the time it was a revolutionary modern design. As the 1970s progressed, variety naturally diminished, but the corporate image perpetuated on the new intakes of Bristol VRTs, Leyland Olympians, and a few oddments such as lightweight Fords and Bedfords, and on the white National coaches. The corporate era was often criticised; to those who remember fondly the pre-1972 liveries, it understandable, but across the NBC there was much to be found of interest. Liveries may have been similar but much else was different, and the origins of each company still made an impression well into the decade; the classic BTC make up of Bristol/ECW differed from the variety often found in former BET companies, both of which contrasted with Midland Red and its homemade vehicles and the still recent independents like West Riding and Gosport & Fareham (Provincial).

In the 1970s many towns had a bus station and garage, though information was not as readily available as today so there was plenty to be discovered. The AM Witton 'Fleetbooks' would be the most readily available reference, and any new vehicles would hopefully be listed in the monthly *Buses* magazine from Ian Allan, as would the numerous inter-company transfers, which often brought variety to otherwise traditional fleets, such as Crosville and the partial North Western amalgamation and United Automobile and its takeover of a number of local independents. Other fleets were already rich in variety, such as Hants & Dorset, City of Oxford and South Wales Transport.

Reference has been made to various PSV Circle fleet histories, Capital Transports' London Country Buses and Green Line Coaches, various official fleet lists (Crosville, Trent, Bristol, Provincial and Hants & Dorset) and enthusiast group fleet lists (PMT, Southdown, Oxford and M&D/East Kent). Readers wishing to see more of the NBC should look at the excellent *A National Bus Company Album* by Ray Stenning, which was the first book devoted to the subject. With a strong design influence and attractive use of maps, it remains one of the finest works on the subject. Other excellent books are *A National Bus Company Album 1981* by D. R. and A. Kennedy, published by OPC, and the two full colour albums *NBC the Early Years* and *NBC: The Road to Privatisation*, both by Kevin Lane and published by Ian Allan. Keith Jenkinson's book *The Final Years of the National Bus Company* has lots of detail about the NBC and in particular on the new fleets that existed briefly in public ownership prior to 1986.

With thousands of vehicles in its ownership, I have attempted to give an impression of what could be found, from the usual to the unusual: the odd service vehicle, along with a few premises' views – always fascinating places, especially in what could be found when visiting an unfamiliar fleet, and in the 1970s permission to look around was easier to obtain.

In the 1970s many routes could trace their origins back in companies' histories. The NBC constituents produced timetables, several in the larger companies, and reference to them today illustrates the once extensive network, including oddments, such as market day-only services or seasonal resort express routes. As the late 1970s dawned changes were on the horizon, driven by a different political agenda. The NBC introduced the Market Analysis Project, or MAP, to study routes and travelling habits. As a result of this a number of localised identities were introduced. Hants & Dorset embraced this scheme, using local names on vinyl over the doors, and Crosville adopted some new local fleets, with the company name incorporated in a smaller font in the design. Following on from the MAP activity, the NBC implemented more extensive restructuring, and new company names began to appear, many on the same livery as before. Much of this was to divide the larger companies; Western National, Midland Red, Hants & Dorset and Bristol Omnibus would be early examples of this in 1983. Eventually all the large companies including United, Crosville, London Country, Eastern Counties and Southdown would be fragmented. Oddly, some small companies such as City of Oxford (Oxford South Midland) would also be split back into its original two organisations. This was an interesting period and I have included some of these new fleet names in the following photographs. In the mid-1980s, with full deregulation approaching there was an explosion of new liveries and fleet names, even some base colours were changed – a new light blue appeared on CAMBUS (formerly part of Eastern Counties). This was to be the twilight era of the National Bus Company as when Devon General (split from Western National) passed into private hands in 1986, the double N symbol would be quickly removed from service buses, only lasting on National Express coaches for a little longer. The outcome of the 1986 deregulation acts is debatable; some companies fared better in the short term than others, though generally change was the only constant. The 'Famous Names' that formed the basis of the government's sales pitch soon disappeared and the days of uniform, neatly painted buses in many areas would be gone for years to come. Unlike British Rail's double-arrow symbol, which still exists today, our double 'N' has disappeared – gone now longer than it existed. There was something comforting in the familiarity of the double N symbol, linking town and country, marketplace and seaside, serving communities in ways that have long since disappeared from everyday life. In this book we take a look back to a very different time, when variety was the norm. Red or green and occasionally blue buses connected us across Wales and England, both urban and rural, serving us all. Together we were really going places.

Alder Valley 350 (MOR 586), Aldershot Bus Station

Taken around 1973, when Aldershot & District and Thames Valley had recently been brought together to become Alder Valley. At this time the new corporate image was being introduced and vehicles from the original two companies could be seen in their original livery but with cream corporate fleet names. 350 was an AEC Reliance new to A&D in 1954 (rebodied by Metro-Cammell in 1967). On the right in a similar vehicle is 343 (HHO 539E), repainted in the new poppy red, and to the rear is a former Alder Valley vehicle in the briefly used dark red livery, which Alder Valley used before poppy red was introduced.

Alder Valley 503 (GPC 729N), Maidenhead Garage, 7 April 1979

A weight restriction on the Thames bridge at Marlow required Alder Valley to operate specific lightweight vehicles. After using second-hand Bristol SULs, in 1974 the company purchased three Leyland EAs fitted with Asco (Ascough Clubman) B19F bodywork made in Dublin. Though unusual, they were not unique as both National Welsh and Bristol (Gloucester) operated similar vehicles.

Alder Valley 760 (SKO 830H), Aldershot Bus Station

Alder Valley's actual title was 'Thames Valley & Aldershot Omnibus Company'. Still in its former owner's livery, 760 (SKO 830H) came from Maidstone & District (3830) in 1974. New in 1970, it was a Daimler SRG6LX with Marshall dual-door bodywork. It would pass to Northern General in 1976.

Alder Valley 44 (FHO 534D), Victoria Coach Station, May 1973

44 was a 1966 AEC Reliance with Metro-Cammell Weymann C49F bodywork. New to Aldershot & District, these stylish coaches were used on the company's express services between London and the towns of Aldershot, Farnham, Guildford and Woking.

Bristol 2401 (922 RAE), Hungerford Station, January 1975

Swindon's 2401, a Bristol MW/ECW, stands at Hungerford railway station ready to work back to its home town. Hungerford was an extremity of the Bristol Omnibus operating area. There was a meeting of City of Oxford, Alder Valley and Hants & Dorset in this border area of Berkshire, Hampshire and Wiltshire.

Bristol W108 (KHU 323P), Bath Garage, June 1985

Bristol Omnibus converted a single Bristol LH in the same style as its earlier Bristol MW Towing conversions. W108 was allocated from new in September 1984 to Bath Garage. It passed to Badgerline in 1986, who painted it in a cream livery with red stripes. Just visible is W12 (GHW 769D), a Land Rover that the company had used for shunting buses at Lawrence Hill. The company owned three such vehicles. Similar W10 (RBO 772) had been allocated to Bath in 1973.

Bristol 2057 (TAE 418G), Bristol City Centre, February 1985

Swindon-allocated Bristol RE 2057 carries its final NBC livery. Swindon & District adopted NBC red in the period before privatisation, Bristol had previously used poppy red on its Cheltenham-allocated local buses in the early 1970s. New in 1969, in a batch numbered 2041–2084 of dual-purpose vehicles, which contained both bus and coach bodywork, 2057 is seen setting out from Bristol on the limited-stop X55 back to north Wiltshire. 2057 was withdrawn in 1985.

Bristol 2063 (WHW 375H), Rupert Street, Bristol, April 1984

Passing the Rupert Street NCP site is Bristol Omnibus dual-purpose Bristol RE 2063. It carries local 'Bath' NBC fleet names, which the company had used both in the early 1970s and again from November 1983. This vehicle passed to Badgerline, who retained its local coach status and lettered it 'Swift Link' in its own version of dual-purpose livery. Bristol Omnibus buses could be seen with City Line, Citybus, Stroud Valleys, Bath, Weston and Wells, Swindon and District, (City of) Gloucester, Cheltenham (District) and Bristol Country Bus fleet names all in NBC corporate style in the mid-1980s.

Cheltenham & Gloucester 3506 (AAE 650V), Gloucester Bus Station, June 1985

The new Cheltenham & Gloucester company used both these locations as fleet names. Leyland National 2 3506 (AAE 650V) was new to Bristol Omnibus in 1980. Later it would carry NBC poppy red with Cheltenham District fleet names complete with the town's civic crest, in the same fashion that Bristol had done in 1973. In the background are two more of the new company's vehicles with Gloucester and Cotswold identities. 'Cotswold' was used on some dual-purpose vehicles operated by the Cheltenham & Gloucester fleet.

Bristol Omnibus Trowbridge Garage/Bus Station

The west Wiltshire town of Trowbridge had been a part of the huge Western National company until 1970, when the NBC transferred its operations in Wiltshire to Bristol Omnibus. Locally allocated 1099 (TAE 148G) waits to depart for Frome, while National South West 256 (DAD 256T), a Leyland Leopard with Plaxton C57F long bodywork, calls on the National 583 service to Portsmouth.

Bristol Omnibus Winterstoke Garage

Bristol VRT 5134 (TWS 915T) stands outside Winterstoke Garage in south Bristol. This garage was built in 1939, but was initially used as a shadow factory for wartime production, resuming its planned role after the war. The garage passed to Cityline with privatisation but later succumbed to redevelopment.

Cheltenham & Gloucester 3084 (JHU 874L), Gloucester Bus Station

Leyland National 3084 had an interesting history. New in 1973, it originally had a dual-door body and carried NBC poppy red and NBC 'Cheltenham' fleet names of the Bristol constituent company. Bristol rebuilt 3084 and 3083 to single-door, fifty-two-seat buses at its own workshops. 3084 is seen in the blue livery with 'City of Gloucester' NBC fleet names adopted by the newly formed Cheltenham and Gloucester Omnibus Company in 1983, though it did use leaf green with simple Gloucester fleet names as well.

Bristol AOU 552V, Marlborough Street Bus Station, Bristol, *c.* 1985

Bristol Omnibus had already been divided into Bristol Country Bus (Badgerline) and Cityline when Ford Escort van AOU 552V was photographed in the exit of the city's large Marlborough Street bus station. Bristol service vehicles were numbered with a W prefix (works fleet) in a series W1–199, though some smaller commercial vehicles omitted the W prefix. AOU 552V's (W fleet number is not known) allocation to which new NBC Bristol company was not clear.

Crosville SMG 497 (6334 FM), Sealand Road Workshops, Chester, 1975

Crosville had a large fleet of Bristol MW vehicles in bus, dual-purpose and coach versions. SMG 497 was a bus seated type. Crosville numbering included a three-letter prefix which indicated information about the vehicle, in this case S – Single; M – Bristol MW; and G – Gardiner engine. Seen in 1975 at the company's central workshops in Chester, it would be allocated to one of the company's Welsh garages, possibly Bangor. Note the newly delivered Bedford TK open service lorry, 62A (OCA 162P).

Crosville SAA 990 (RDB 837), Macclesfied Bus Garage, 1975

The former North Western Road Car Company stage operations had been divided by the NBC between Ribble, Crosville and SELNEC (Greater Manchester PTE) in 1972. Crosville received two garages and an interesting selection of vehicles, many of which were non-standard to the largely Bristol/ECW fleet of Crosville. New in 1961, formerly NWRCC 837, SAA 990 was an AEC Reliance with Alexander dual-purpose bodywork. Though retaining coach seats, Crosville classified it as a bus. Crosville would only get three years of service before its withdrawal in 1975.

Crosville ENL 913 (NCA 973N), Chester, 1975

For its vast operating area, Crosville owned a large fleet of dual-purpose Leyland Nationals. One of these was ENL 913, seen arriving at Chester bus station at the end of the long L1 'Cymru Coastliner' service from Caernarfon, a distance of 70 miles. The coach-seated Leyland Nationals were well suited for this type of duty, though Crosville would later use downgraded coaches for these services.

Crosville CVT 683 (NFM 683E)

Crosville was a Tilling company with a majority Bristol/ECW fleet in the 1960s. The purchase of a small number of lightweight Bedford coaches in the 1960s was unusual. Fourteen were purchased in 1967/69 with both Duple and Plaxton C45F bodywork. Mostly allocated to the company's Welsh garages, they suited tour work that Crosville operated from the holiday towns of North Wales, though CVT 683 had been pressed into National Express work when seen in the mid-1970s. Though classed as coaches by the company, it had painted them all in local coach livery in 1972/73, though latterly painted all in National coach white livery.

Crosville DFG 257 (SFM 257G), Crewe Garage, June 1977

DFG 257 was a typical Crosville vehicle. The company had large numbers of Bristol Lodekkas, in both front- and rear-door versions. DFG 257 was allocated to Crewe garage, and several were still in use there into the 1980s. Alongside is EPG 724, one of the unusual Seddon Pennine vehicles that the company bought in the early 1970s, possibly as a result of vehicle shortages. The vehicles are parked outside the garage building which faced the town's bus station, a 1960s purpose-built facility that sadly no longer exists.

Cumberland 231 (AAO 34B)

Cumberland was one of NBC's smallest constituents and served mainly the coastal towns in the county, with Ribble operating through the parts of Lake District and the areas around Carlisle and Penrith. Cumberland was a former Tilling company and, apart from a few coaches, mainly used Bristol/ECW vehicles in early NBC days. 231 was a Bristol MW with bus seats new in 1964. It was seen parked at one of the company's outstations, a common arrangement at the time to avoid unnecessary running back to garages.

Cumberland 607 (ACH 142H), Keswick Bus Station

607 was a former 1972 Trent Leyland Leopard/Plaxton C40F, one of four transferred from Trent to Cumberland for contact duties with a route that had vehicle length restrictions. This vehicle would last into the early 1990s with Stagecoach, being reregistered as RSR 846H. Cumberland never had many dual-purpose vehicles in the 1970s – a single Bristol RE and a small number of lightweight coaches occasionally painted in local coach livery.

Cumberland Whitehaven Garage, c. 1984

Cumberland had its headquarters in Whitehaven where its garage (seventy-five vehicles), bus station and central workshops covered a large area near the railway station. In this view a number of Leyland Nationals, including both later series 2 and short B series types, and a Leyland Willowbrook 003 in 'Boarder Clipper' livery, await their next duties.

Cumberland Workington Garage, c. 1984

Cumberland's second largest garage was at Workington (thirty-five vehicles). This 1984 view shows both Bristol VRTs and Leyland National series 2s, which at this time formed large parts of the fleet. Nearest to the camera is 417 (FAO 417V), a 1979 Bristol VRTSL6G. The company had a close association with the Leyland National as it was manufactured just outside the town.

East Kent (575 RKJ), Maidstone Bus Station, 1974

East Kent was unusual in not using fleet numbers for its vehicles in early NBC days; identification was by the registration plate numbers. 575 was a Leyland Atlantean with Metro-Cammell bodywork. It was new to Maidstone & District in 1961, being transferred to East Kent in 1974. Newly repainted, it stands next to Maidstone & District 3281 (281 DKT), an AEC Reliance with Weymann body, still in original M&D livery. These two fleets enjoyed close co-operation, and vehicle exchanges were common.

East Kent (AFN 765B), Canterbury Bus Station

AEC Regent V/Park Royal '765' of 1964 passes Canterbury bus station in 1974. The majority of vehicles are in the new poppy red livery. Note the East Kent mini service van P162 (BFN 455K) in unmarked blue livery.

East Kent 7342 (VUF 324K), Dover Garage, 1984

By the time this photograph was taken of this ex-Southdown Northern Counties-bodied Daimler Fleetline, East Kent had adopted fleet numbers in a series with neighbouring Maidstone & District. 7342 had come to East Kent from Southdown in 1981, and a number were painted in contract liveries for transfers to cross-Channel shipping, such as Hoverspeed or P&O Ferries.

East Kent (WFN 503), Canterbury Bus Station

East Kent had a number of AEC Reliances fitted with Park Royal dual-purpose bodywork. WFN 503 had gained NBC local coach livery, while others were finished in NBC poppy red bus livery but retained coach seating. Unusually a number were fitted with canoe roof racks.

Mansfield District A805 (FNN 162D), Mansfield Garage, 24 July 1975

The NBC amalgamated the East Midland and Mansfield District fleet in 1972, and in the process NBC green was adopted for both fleets, though individual fleet names were retained. The vehicles were numbered in a common series and a prefix letter was used to identify the type and fleet allocation: 'A' being Mansfield District single-deck, 'B' Mansfield District double-deck, 'C' East Midland Coach, 'D' East Midland double-deck, 'MC' Mansfield District coach and 'S' East Midland single-deck. No separate code was used for dual-purpose vehicles, which used C and MC. A805 (FNN 162D) was a Bristol MW6G of 1966, in a batch of six (A801–6) which included four from Midland General.

East Midland S403 (403 RRR), Doncaster Bus Station

S403, a Leyland Leopard/Willowbrook B53F, was typical of the East Midland fleet. East Midland was a former BET group company and Mansfield District was a BTC company, so the combined fleet reflected the differing vehicle purchases of the two companies.

East Midland C70 (270 UVO), Sheffield, 1973

C70 was an AEC Reliance with Willowbrook DP49F bodywork, seen working a British Rail staff shuttle to the large Diesel Traction Depot at Tinsley. It was in a batch of ten new in 1964, but was sold in the mid-1970s to a Scottish independent. The rest of the batch lasted a little longer with East Midland.

Mansfield District 175 (175 NVO), Mansfield Garage

175 was an Albion Lowlander with Alexander bodywork. East Midland/Mansfield District transferred vehicles between the fleets so vehicles of BET origins could receive Mansfield District fleet names, a fleet more associated with Bristol/ECW products. This vehicle was D175 with East Midland NBC fleet names. Later renumbered 275, it was withdrawn in the late 1970s and was preserved for a time.

East Midland S392 (392 LRR) and S389 (389 HRR), Chesterfield Workshops

Typical East Midland vehicles, two Leyland Leopards with BET-style bodywork. S392 was from Marshall and S389 was Willowbrook in 1962 and 1961 respectively, both recently repainted from East Midlands livery of dark red and cream. Both would see further use with independents north of the border.

East Midland 524 (DWF 24V), Retford Garage, 1985

Leyland Leopard 524 (DWF 24V) is not as it appears. New in a batch of five with Willowbrook 003 bodies, East Midland had them rebodied in 1985 as buses, four by Duple, and this one resulting in a unique Leyland Leopard/Alexander P-type combination. At this time the NBC livery was being relaxed and the white line is applied in a non-standard fashion.

East Yorkshire 877 (RKH 877G), York

East Yorkshire had an interesting collection of standard BET-bodied dual-purpose vehicles. 877 was a Leyland Leopard with Marshall DP49F body. This vehicle had been painted in NBC blue local coach livery in 1973, before the company changed to standard NBC poppy red livery. 877 is seen in York whilst working the 44 service from Bridlington to Leeds.

East Yorkshire's Hull Garage, May 1984

Neighbouring Lincolnshire Bristol VRT 1967 (SVL 177W) stands over outside East Yorkshire's large garage in Hull (100 vehicles) along with an EYMS coach, 207 (XAG 207X), a Willowbrook-bodied Leyland Leopard. The VRT had probably travelled from Scunthorpe, where the vehicle was allocated in the early 1980s.

East Yorkshire 927 (DKH 927L), Hull Paragon Railway Station, *c.* 1974

An interesting view of the bus park, alongside Hull Paragon station, with Bristol VRT 927, which was delivered in traditional East Yorkshire dark blue. Behind is dual-purpose vehicle 770 in the short-lived NBC blue variation used by the company. Alongside is 846 (MAT 846F), a Leyland Leopard/Marshall DP49F with a non-standard front grille, which has received NBC poppy red, which was adopted when the NBC directed against the use of NBC blue.

Eastern Countries LM970 (8009 VF), Cambridge Garage, 20 July 1978

Eastern Counties, as a former BTC fleet, had a mainly Bristol/ECW fleet when the NBC was formed. Inside Cambridge garage in July 1978 were all Bristol/ECW products including X55 (46 CNG), the locally allocated Bristol FLF towing vehicle. Central is LM970 (8009 VF), a typical bus-bodied example. New in 1962 (LM470), it served with the company until 1977 when it was sold for scrap. The company had operated over 150 Bristol MWs in both bus and coach specifications.

Eastern Countries LS775 (VVF 775), Norwich, 1974

Eastern Counties had one of the largest operating areas in the NBC, covering Norfolk, Suffolk and Cambridgeshire. In the 1970s, apart from Leyland Nationals, a few Bedford and Leyland Leopard coaches and various minibuses, the majority of its fleet was Bristol/ECW vehicles. The Eastern Coach Works was located in Lowestoft, and the company had a close association with the body builder. The company used a two/three-letter prefix system to identify its vehicles. LS775 was a 1957 Bristol LS5G with an ECW C39F body. It had been downgraded to dual purpose and had been converted for one-man operation. It was withdrawn in 1975.

Eastern Counties Central Workshops, Norwich, 1973

At a time when the corporate NBC livery was introduced, two ECOC Bristols stand newly repainted outside the company's central workshops in Cremorne Lane, Norwich. Bristol VRT VR318 (OCS 578H) was one of the vehicles involved in the NBC/Scottish Bus Group VRT/FLF exchanges of 1973. Eastern Counties took thirty Bristol VRTs. This one came from Western SMT (2248), while alongside is an original Eastern Counties vehicle, Bristol RE coach RE877 (AAH 125B). Note the short-lived small underlined fleet name application above the front wheel.

Eastern Counties MB998 (KCL 416N)

At a time when a minibus was rare in any NBC fleet, Eastern Counties operated a small number for dedicated rural services, often in cooperation with local country councils. MB998 was a Ford Transit with twelve-seat Deansgate bodywork. The NBC had issued a diagram using half-red/white local coach livery for minibuses, which was used irrespective of the type used by most NBC companies with such vehicles.

Eastern Counties Southwold Garage, 1974

With a huge operating area, Eastern Counties maintained numerous small garages and outstations. The small garage (four vehicles) at Southwold was typical of the smaller buildings used by the company. A sub-garage of Lowestoft, it was located in Station Road and would close in September 1983, after which vehicles were parked outdoors at various locations around the small town. The LS790 (5790 AH), a Bristol MW/ECW C39F new in 1959 (as C32F), was rebuilt by ECW for one-man operation in January 1970, retaining its roof-level windows. Repainted in NBC dual-purpose livery in August 1973, it would be withdrawn in 1975.

Eastern National 2889 (WNO 977F), Colchester Garage

With an operating area of Essex, a small part of Hertfordshire and a garage in East London, for much of the 1970s Eastern National was made up entirely of Bristol and Leyland National vehicles, apart from a handful of second-hand double-deck Guy Arabs and five Ford R1014s with Duple Dominant bus bodies. The fleet carried two-letter allocation plates in the same style as the fleet number plate. Bristol FLF 2889 shows its allocation as CR (Colchester). Eastern National operated the last Bristol FLF built in its fleet.

Eastern National 1600 (BNO 101B), Southend, 4 April 1976

Eastern National had a batch of twelve coach-bodied dual-purpose Bristol REs delivered in 1964/70. Under the NBC all but two were painted as buses in NBC leaf green and a number, including 1600, also gained bus seats, which was unusual for this type of body. 1600 (BNO 101B) was allocated to Southend garage (SD), and is seen along with two similar buses and a Bristol MW in its home town in April 1976.

Eastern National 1610 (GVW 980H), Chelmsford Bus Station

One of the two dual-purpose livered Bristol REs, 1610 (GVW 980H), mentioned opposite, is seen at its home bus station in the late 1970s. With few express services at this time these were the only local coach liveried vehicles in the fleet. Note the application of the NBC logo, which should be centred above the front wheel, leaving a large gap before the fleet name. Oddly, many NBC ENOC vehicles had slightly non-standard applications of the corporate fleet name.

Eastern National 1419 (GJD 195N), Chelmsford Central Workshops

For much of the 1970s Eastern National operated no white National coaches. These operations were undertaken by Samuelsons, Timpsons, Tillings or later National Travel South East. In 1979 Eastern National regained its coaching activities. 1419 was a Bristol RE/Plaxton new to National Travel South East. Later it gained a new front panel and the company painted it in NBC Venetian blind dual-purpose livery. In 1985 it was transferred to Bristol (Badgerline) 2085, reregistered CSV 618, in the company's 'Swift Link' white, yellow and green scheme.

Hants & Dorset 630 (CRU 140L), Swanage Bus Station

Hants & Dorset had a large fleet of Bristol REs with ECW dual-door bodywork. Some had entered the fleet from Wilts & Dorset when these two fleets were fully amalgamated in October 1972. 630 (CRU 630L) dates from 1972, and had been allocated to Salisbury when new. Devoid of the white relief band, when photographed it was displaying the white/brown dots to indicate its allocation to Swanage garage. With the split of the company into Hampshire Bus and Wilts & Dorset in 1983, 630 founds itself in the Poole-based Wilts & Dorset company.

Wilts & Dorset 1646 (UEL 566J), Salisbury Bus Station, August 1984

With new Wilts & Dorset NBC fleet names from the formation of the new company the year before, Bristol RE 1646 in dual-purpose livery awaits departure from Salisbury's bus station, a location that did survive privatisation but has sadly since been redeveloped. In the background is Leyland Olympian/ECW 3903 (A903 JPR) fitted with coach seating, one of the first vehicles purchased new by Wilts & Dorset after the division of Hants & Dorset.

Provincial 39 (MHO 190F), Hoeford Garage, 19 June 1977

One of the smallest NBC constituents, Provincial was the trading name for Gosport & Fareham Omnibus Company, which had been independent up to 1970. After nationalisation the company was closely associated with Hants & Dorset. 39 (MHO 190F) was a Seddon Pennine IV with Strachan dual-door bodywork, from a batch of five new in 1968, a type not found elsewhere in the NBC. (D. Mant)

Lincolnshire 1667 (KVL 453L), Grimsby Garage

An unusual combination within the NBC was a Bristol LH/ECW finished as a dual-purpose vehicle. 1667 was new in 1970, so has the early flat front. A number of this batch had the shallow windscreen, which were rebuilt by ECW to give better driver visibility. Lincolnshire had one of the largest fleets of Bristol LHs in the NBC. They replaced Bristol SC4LKs, some of which lasted into corporate livery. 1667 was withdrawn in 1982.

Lincolnshire 2535 (DFE 961D), Scunthorpe Bus Garage

Bristol Lodekka FS5G 2535 (DFE 961D) departs from the combined location of bus station/garage in Scunthorpe. Like many other NBC fleets from Tilling/BTC origins, vehicles were mostly Bristol/ECW, along with the usual Leyland Nationals, but a small number of Ford R1014 with Duple bus bodies were purchased in 1976. Note the company's Ford Escort service van in the background.

Lincolnshire 1052 (YVL 836S), Newark Bus Station, August 1984

With the company's garage in the background Bristol LH/ECW 1362 (YVL 836S) carries local identity fleet names 'East Notts Lincolnshire', which were introduced as a result of MAP studies – also illustrating the odd fact that the company had a garage in Nottinghamshire! Another Bristol LH (but with a Marshal body) of the well-known local independent W. Gash & Sons is parked in the background. Newark also hosted Mansfield District services.

London Country RP83 (JPA 183K), July 1974

London Country faced vehicle issues when it was formed in 1970. One of the most pressing issues was its extensive, prestigious 'Green Line' network, as many of the vehicles inherited were no longer suitable. The NBC company ordered ninety AEC Reliance with Park Royal C45F bodies to replace RCS, RCLs and RMCs Routemasters. As delivered, the RPs were painted in the pre-corporate Lincoln green livery. With the introduction of corporate livery they were all painted in dual-purpose livery. NBC allowed the use of Green Line corporate fleet names, though oddly on RPs the names were carried in white on the side as opposed to green on the roof above the windows. RP83 is seen on the long 727 Luton to Crawley service. Later the RPs would be demoted to bus livery.

London Country RMC 4 (SLT 59), Welwyn Garden City Bus Station, April 1978

Looking a little incongruous in NBC leaf green, Hertford garages RMC4 was a prototype Routemaster coach, with unique ECW bodywork. London Country had been formed in 1970 from London Transport 'green' country areas. The new NBC company had over 1,200 vehicles, making it one the three largest NBC constituents. Initially the vehicles were all usual London Transport types, so AEC Regals, Swifts and Routemasters all appeared in NBC corporate liveries.

London Country SM 129 (BPH 129H)

Another typical London Transport type seen in NBC leaf green. AEC Swift SM 129 (BPH 129H) had always been green. Delivered in Country area dark green in 1970, it gained NBC livery in July 1973. A long-term resident of Addleston garage, it finished its service as a trainer at Windsor in September 1979, before being sold in 1980.

London Country SNC138 (XPG 238N), Croydon Bus Station, 17 September 1977

After a small batch of AEC Swifts/Alexanders for Green Line work, London Country took delivery of Leyland Nationals in large numbers. The first ones to be allocated to Green Line work were the 11.3-metre versions classed as LNC (Long National Coach), but early LNCs were fitted with bus-type seats, so they should have been classed LNB (Bus), therefore making them unsuitable for their planned work. To address this, the company re-covered the seats using LT-style blue and green moquette. Later deliveries were the shorter 10.3-metre type (SNC), which were fitted with the correct coach-style seating from new. Seen in 1977 at Croydon is SNC138 of Chelsham (CM) garage. The correct high-backed coach seats are visible. The company eventually decided that the use of Leyland Nationals did not help promote the Green Line network and subsequently used grant specification coach types in a revised livery.

London Country P5 (SPK 205M), June 1974

The first coaches with London Country to carry National white livery was a batch of five AEC Reliance with Plaxton Panorama Elite C49F bodies. New in 1973, these were joined in 1976 by two more with earlier-style bodies from National Travel South East. These seven were the only coaches in the fleet to carry Central Activities Group white livery. This batch would be painted in Green Line livery from 1978, along with coaches from National Travel London transferred to cover former Maidstone & District tour work around Gravesend, when that company closed its garage in 1978. In the early 1980s the companies would become involved in the National Express network and coaches in NBC Venetian blind livery on a white base with red Green Line names introduced.

Maidstone & District 3281 (281 DKT), Maidstone Bus Station, 1974

Maidstone & District applied NBC Corporate fleet names on its traditional dark green livery. Initially the NBC had instructed new fleet names could be applied on existing liveries but using cream transfers. This was short-lived and it was preferred that companies waited until vehicles were fully repainted and white transfers used. In contradiction, 3281 has had white fleet names applied.

Maidstone & District 6089 (89 YKT), Maidstone Bus Station, 1974

Another vehicle seen at the time of change, 6089 was a Northern Counties-bodied Daimler Fleetline from 1963. The surrounding vehicles were all in new corporate livery. This batch of vehicles would receive NBC green livery. A number of similar vehicles went to East Kent in NBC poppy red.

Maidstone & District 5869 (FKM 869V), Gillingham Garage, 1983

Enthusiasts would have no problem identifying Maidstone & District Bristol VRT 5869 with its roof-applied number. 5869 was new in 1979 and was fitted with a low-height body. The company also operated the high-bridge version as well. Note the company's Ford Transit service van, P84 (CKK 284T), in National white livery. Maidstone & District had painted its vans in leaf green, often with the side panel in white. By the 1980s, many NBC companies would keep the factory colours for these vehicles to save money.

Maidstone & District Bexhill Garage

Built in 1970, Leyland Leopard/Marshall B45F 3411 (UKE 411H) stands outside Bexhill garage (twenty vehicles), which was located within the Southern Region Sussex coastline at the rear and faced the closed Bexhill West terminus station across the road. Photographs of garage locations are always interesting. This garage closed in April 1980, succumbing, like many others, to commercial development.

Midland Red 5914 (PHA 514G), Hinkley Garage, 1975

Midland Red was unique in the NBC with its home-built vehicles. 5914 (PHA 514G), a type S22, classed as DP45F, was designed for longer-distance services. The batch followed on from type S21, which the company designated as a semi-coach, distinct from the dual-purpose term used for the S22. The BMMO-built appearance was stylish, if a little austere. 5914 was new in October 1968 to Evesham. It moved to Hinkley in 1971, where it was seen in 1974. Its final allocation was Worcester from December 1976 until it was withdrawn in June 1980.

Midland Red 5960 (UHA 960H), Stafford, June 1979

5960 (UHA 960H) was classed as S23 by the company with B51F bodywork. The S23 was a batch of seventy-six vehicles (5916–5991) built between 1968 and 1970; 5942–5991 were finished off by Plaxton, but the design was still BMMO. This batch contained 5991, which was the last BMMO-constructed vehicle. Twenty-four S23s passed to WMPTE in December 1973. The last two S23s, 5930/5937, were withdrawn from Rugby in February 1981. These were also the last BMMO-built vehicles in MROC use. 5960 was withdrawn in June 1980 from Stafford garage.

Midland Red 360 (GOH 360N), Stafford Garage, c. 1980

Midland Red Leyland Leopard (MROC type SDP28) 360 has just left its home garage in Stafford with a service to Litchfield. Midland Red had purchased 152 dual-purpose Leyland Leopards after the company ceased building and finishing its own vehicles. Early deliveries had Willowbrook bodies, while later ones had similar Marshall bodywork, and all were DP49F. They were a common sight across the Midlands, often working the long express journeys between towns as far apart as Malvern, Shrewsbury, Leicester and Banbury. This type of vehicle was used for NBC's very first application of dual-purpose livery in 1972.

Midland Red 6233 (WHA 233H), Western National Radipole Garage, 1973

Seen outside the Western National Radipole Garage near Weymouth, Midland Red 6233 was a Leyland Leopard/Plaxton Panorama 1 new in 1970 to Swadlincote garage. Midland Red allocated its type code LC11. A batch of thirty, they were delivered in the company's dark red livery, although it received National white livery in NBC ownership. It would serve in this livery until withdrawal in 1980. Midland Red also painted the very first National white coach, applied to a CM6T Motorway coach in 1972.

Midland Red Evesham Garage, *c.* 1984

With an allocation of thirteen vehicles, Midland Red's Evesham Garage was in use by Midland Red West when this photograph was taken in 1984. Midland Red was one of the largest NBC constituents (with over 1,000 vehicles) and was forced to divide into four operating areas in 1981 in preparation for privatisation. Inside the garage are a Leyland National and a Leyland Leopard similar to 360, seen above. Midland Red West continued to operate after deregulation in an attractive red/cream livery but eventually disappeared into the large fleets that dominated operations today.

Midland Red 670 (RDA 670R), Burton-on-Trent Bus Station

To replace its dual-purpose Leyland Leopards already mentioned, Midland Red purchased grant specification Leyland Leopards with Plaxton Supreme Express bodywork. 670 was in a batch of eighteen from 1977/78, classed type code C18. They were delivered in standard NBC red/white dual-purpose livery. 670 was allocated to Tamworth when new, but was reclassified as CDP18 in 1980, passing to Midland Red North in 1981. MRN used regional names depending on the vehicle's allocation, Mercian being used at Tamworth garage. In the early 1980s, the four Midland Red NBC companies (and United Counties) developed the Midland Express network, all using the same livery to promote these services.

Midland Red South 64 (SAD 127R), Stratford-upon-Avon Garage

Midland Red South 64 (SAD 127R) is seen in its home garage wearing 'Stratford Blue' fleet names in the contemporary NBC Venetian blind livery. 64 was a Leyland Leopard with the striking Willowbrook Spacecar bodywork. It was new to National Travel South West (Black & White) fleet as 127/427. Stratford-upon-Avon Garage had previously been one of two Stratford Blue depots, the other being at Kineton. The company had been part of Midland Red since 1935, though it kept its identity up until 1972, when it was absorbed into the Midland Red NBC identity. The 1980 saw its name revived for some Midland Red South services.

Midland Red 5615 (BHA 615C), Worcester Bus Station, mid-1970s

An early evening view of the Worcester bus station, which was sited near to the River Severn in the 1970s. BMMO S17 5615 (BHA 615C) and BMMO D9 5319 (6319 HA) are crossing on the long 144 service from Birmingham to the Malverns/Worcester via Droitwich Spa. Another D9, 4899 (899 KHA), works a Worcester local service. On the left are two non-BMMO types.

Northern General (Gateshead) 2923 (LCH 523K), Benton Estate, January 1975

Another Gateshead lettered vehicle, 2923 (later 4257) was a Daimler Fleetline SRG6 with a Willowbrook body, a chassis usually used for double-deck vehicles. The Northern General had an interesting fleet and operated a number of types not found elsewhere within the NBC.

Northern General/United, Hartlepool Bus Station, March 1975

Though a number of Northern General buses are present, Hartlepool was in United Automobile territory. Sunderland District used a blue livery, though a different shade to East Yorkshire and Midland General for a brief period in the early 1970s. Also using Daimler Fleetline SRG6 chassis, 388 (LUP 388J) with an Alexander W-type body wears the rare NBC blue livery complete with corporate lettering. Alongside is 3074 (RCN 690), an AEC/Park Royal 'Routemaster', and 4124 (BCN 503C), an AEC Reliance/Weymann DP49F still in Northern General red/cream livery. Just visible behind is a United Bristol RE 6086 (DNH 686N).

Northern General South Shields Garage, March 1981

Northern General ordered the unusual Marshall Camair for some of its Leyland Panthers, the only NBC constituent to operate them. A few had passed to Midland Red from Stratford Blue and even repainted in red, but they saw no use before being sold. NGT had taken delivery of twenty-five for use in a number of its subsidiary fleets. Delivered as dual-door, the company rebuilt them to single door. Two are seen here: 4144 (GCN 847G) and driver trainer T431, ex-4112, (GCN 845G) along with a good selection of Northern General types, in both poppy red and PTE yellow.

Northern General 3245 (OTY 404M), Sunderland Garage, mid-1970s

Still in Sunderland District blue livery Leyland Atlantean/Park Royal 3245 (OTY 404M) has gained Northern fleet names, probably around 1975 when the Sunderland & District fleet name was discontinued. This type was also used by London Country/Ribble/Yorkshire and Southdown and this vehicle went to London Country South West in the mid-1980s.

Northern General 4361 (9534 PT), Sunderland Garage, mid-1970s

Visible in the background in the photo above, a rare view of Northern General Leyland Leopard L1 tow bus conversion 4361 (9534 PT), which had been cut back after the rear axle. Interestingly it was not numbered in the service fleet, simply retaining its bus number. This bus had been 234 in the Venture fleet in NBC poppy red livery. Converted in July 1976, it was recorded as allocated to Philadelphia Garage (*sic*).

Northern General (Tynemouth) 332 (GAT 819D), Percy Main Garage, January 1976

AEC Renown 332 was former East Yorkshire 819, part a batch of six which was exchanged for Daimler Fleetlines in early 1972, in the Tynemouth fleet. Renumbered 3210 in 1975 when Tynemouth was absorbed into the main Northern General fleet, some of the batch received NBC poppy red livery, though Tynemouth had repainted most in the PTE area yellow livery.

Northern General 3079 (RCN 695)

The AEC Routemaster was unfamiliar outside the capital. Northern General though took delivery of fifty-two in the front entrance version including ex-London Transport (RMF1254), which was the prototype front entrance Routemaster (NGT number 2145/3129). The company modified two others: 'Tynesider' (3000) with a prominent engine bonnet and the 'Wearsider' (3069), both to enable one-man operation. Only two NGT Routemaster were painted in NBC yellow, and all had been withdrawn by 1980.

Northern General Philadelphia Garage, 26 August 1984

Northern General group's largest garage was at Philadelphia (Houghton-le-Spring), housing seventy-one vehicles. This garage was used by Sunderland District and had formerly been the depot for Sunderland District Electric Tramways until the system was abandoned in 1925. Retained for the replacement buses, it survived until recently being closed by Go North East after 113 years' service. A collection of Leyland Nationals, Bristol VRTs and Leyland Atlantean in poppy red and T&WPTE yellow typify the fleet at this period when only the Northern fleet names were in use.

Northern General Consett Garage, 26 August 1984

Seen on the same day as above, Consett's garage in Leadgate Road, which had an allocation of fifty-eight vehicles (in 1982), has a collection of Leyland Nationals outside when seen in 1984 including 4534 (MGR 534P) and 4512 (PCN 427M), both with B49F bodywork. Northern General had a large fleet of Leyland Nationals, including some of the earliest delivered in 1972. By 1978 it had approximately 200 in the fleet.

Northern General (Gateshead) 78 (HCN 478)

This 1958 Leyland PD3/4 with MCW Orion bodywork was still in service long enough to receive the NBC yellow livery used on buses in the Tyne & Wear PTE area. Northern General retained its sub-fleet names into the corporate era. Gateshead, Tynemouth, Tyneside, Sunderland District and Venture could be seen in the early 1970s, though the names were phased out by 1975 (Gateshead/Tyneside in 1976).

Oxford South Midland 47 (RTJ 364G), Wantage, 1977

47 (RTJ 364G) was a Plaxton-bodied Ford R192 which had come from Midland Red in 1975. In turn they had acquired the business of Hoggins of Wrockwardine Wood (a village near Telford) in 1974. It was in a pair with 48 (AAW 471K). Oxford added the destination box and painted it in NBC local coach livery. Hoggins had purchased this vehicle from Sharrock of Westhoughton (Lancs), number 2180 by Midland Red, though they never used this vehicle in service. The 302 service operated from Didcot/Wantage to Oxford.

Oxford South Midland 793 (793 TJO), Gloucester Green Bus Station, Oxford, 1973

Oxford also applied corporate fleet names to its well-liked pre-NBC livery. This AEC Reliance/Willowbrook B44F of 1964 waits service at Oxford bus station. It would later receive standard poppy red bus livery. Oxford South Midland was unique amongst the NBC constituents in that it did not operate the Leyland National.

Oxford South Midland Bicester Garage, c. 1974

City of Oxford Motor Service had one large garage/workshop in Cowley Road, Oxford, and several other garages that were all small, some having allocations in single figures. With an allocation of twelve, Bicester's small garage was located in London Road adjacent to a level crossing. Here is Bristol VRT 903 and Ford R1014 with Willowbrook body 642.

Oxford South Midland 1 (DFC 601D), Oxford, 1975

City of Oxford Motor Services carried Oxford South Midland fleet names and had a small but fascinating fleet with small numbers of different types. Oxford 1 (DFC 601D) was an AEC Reliance/Duple Northern (Commander III) C45F built in 1966. Like many of its coaches, Oxford painted them in NBC local coach livery. Originally this vehicle carried Oxford's attractive maroon and duck-egg green livery. The company had fitted the roof destination box.

Potteries 135 (WEH 135G)

PMT took delivery of fifty-eight Daimler Roadliners (with both Plaxton and Marshall bodies) and six coach versions (three Plaxton Panorama C1097–C1099 and three Duple Commander C1100–C1102), making it the largest operator of the type. The last ten were delivered in 1969 with Plaxton dual-door bodywork (130–139). They were the first buses to not carry Potteries prefix letters to the fleet number. The Roadliners was not a successful design and the company disposed of them by the mid-1970s, the coach versions lasting only four years.

Potteries 219 (PVT 219L), Newcastle Garage, 1974

PMT had some unusual single-deck vehicles when the NBC was formed, including Alexander W-bodied Daimler Fleetlines and the problematic Daimler 'Roadliner', along with usual BET-bodied types. After a history of variety by the late 1970s the fleet was standardised on Leyland Leopards and Nationals with Bristol REs and VRTs. 219 (PVT 219L) was a Bristol RELL6L/ECW B53F of 1972. The company also had the shorter RESL version.

Potteries 167 (DVT 167J), Birmingham, 1975

Seen near Moor Street in central Birmingham, PMT 167 (DVT 167J) was an Alexander Y type but was fitted to the less usual AEC Reliance chassis. Following on from twelve delivered in 1967/68, 167 was in a batch of thirteen delivered in 1970/71, some of which had a restyled front.

Potteries 36 (XEH 136M), Longton Bus Station

Potteries (PMT) only operated a small number of white-livered National coaches, but it did have numerous dual-purpose vehicles. After the Y-type vehicles seen opposite, the company took delivery of 'Grant Coaches' such as Ford R1014/Duple C45F 36 (XEH 136M). A batch of seven from 1973/74, it was painted in NBC local-coach livery from new. PMT also owned the longer Duple coach body version, also in this livery. PMT also had three dual purpose Bristol RE/ECWs and later a small number of Leyland National 2s with coach seating.

Potteries 862 (862 REH), Newcastle Garage

PMT operated eighty-seven Leyland Atlanteans with low-height Weymann bodies. They formed the majority of the double-deck fleet. From 1974 the company took delivery of Bristol VRTs, initially forty-three vehicles. 862 stands inside Newcastle garage, which also acted as a Crosville outstation. With seventy-one vehicles, only Hanley had a larger allocation.

Potteries 1006 (5006 VT), Newcastle Bus Station

A Bristol RE Alexander Y type, Leyland National and Bristol VRTs form a typical selection of PMT vehicles in the mid-1970s, seen in this view of 1006 leaving Newcastle bus station. 1006, with 1002 alongside, were Daimler Fleetlines with Alexander bodywork, in a batch of thirty-four from 1964/65.

Potteries 719 (MFA 719V), Stoke Woodhouse Street Garage/Workshops

A new Bristol VRT is seen outside PMT garage/main workshops in Woodhouse Street, Stoke. This location closed as running garage in 1980 when it had an allocation of forty-three vehicles. Note the two Ford Transit PMT service vans in the background – a company's main workshop was a good location to find these rare vehicles. Apart from a small number of NBC trial vehicles the company only took Bristol VRTs after 1974 for its double-deck intake.

Potteries L9786 (786 EVT), Stoke, July 1974

PMT keenly applied the corporate fleet name to its vehicles whilst in pre-NBC livery. L9786, a Leyland Atlantean with Weymann H39/34F low-bridge bodywork. still retains its earlier fleet number. PMT renumbered it 786 *c.* 1973.

Potteries 10 (MRE 138B), Stoke-on-Trent, 1973

Potteries Motor Traction, or PMT as it was known, had a small geographic operating area, with the majority of its garages within the six towns. In 1982 it had a fleet of 351. Its earlier vehicle history was full of vehicles taken over from local independents, but by the NBC era only a handful survived including Albion Victor/ Duple Firefly 10 (MRE 138B), formerly with Staniers of Newchapel, remaining in the fleet just long enough to receive an NBC logo. It was sold in 1974.

Ribble 1024 (WTF 570L), Blackpool Devonshire Road Garage, June 1985

Ribble operated two garages in Blackpool. The larger one in Devonshire Road was also used by Standerwick/ National Travel West. 1024 was a Leyland Leopard/Duple C49F. It was new in National white livery with Ribble fleet names, but had been downgraded to dual-purpose when seen here.

Ribble 1095 (YFR 495R), Blackpool Coliseum Coach Station

The Coliseum coach station in Blackpool was a mecca for visiting NBC coaches in the 1970s/80s. Vehicles from numerous NBC constituents could be seen parked against the backdrop of the town's tram depot, though Ribble's 1095 and 813 could have stood over in their own company's garages in the town!

Ribble 1285 (RRN 434), Clitheroe Garage

The white glass gives a clue to Leyland Atlantean 1285's origins. New in 1962, it was one of Ribble's twenty prestigious 'White Ladys' with an extra luggage rack fitted to these double-deck coaches. 1285 displays the X23 route blind, for the Clitheroe to Manchester service, a common service for these vehicles.

Ribble 1484 (TRN 484V), Carlisle

The ECW-bodied Daimler Fleetline always looked a little unusual. 1484 also had a high-bridge body; the proportions of the bodywork, particularly the thickness of the white line paint above the cab, is an indicator of this bodywork variation. 1484 (TRN 484V) operates an exact fare only service out of Carlisle in the early 1980s.

Ribble Carlisle Garage NT East (OKY 52R)

National Travel East Willowbrook 'Spacecar' OKY 52R makes use of Ribble's garage in Carlisle while on tour work. With one large nationalised organisation, economy and cooperation like this was possible. Ribble operated a fairly standard fleet in the NBC era, though it did own a large number of full-fronted half-cab double-deck vehicles: Leyland Titans with Burlington and MCW bodies and Albion Lowlander with similar Alexander bodywork.

Ribble 618 (CCK 618C), Penrith Garage

Leyland Leopard 618 was a typical Ribble single-deck bus. The company owned over 200 with similar BET-style bodies from Marshall and Weymann. 618 had a Weymann B53F body and was seen outside Penrith garage in the mid-1970s.

Ribble 811 (ARN 811C), Ambleside Garage, 1977

Ribble 811 (ARN 811C) receives a wash in the company's Ambleside garage, which was situated with the town's bus station, though at a lower level. Ribble was one of the largest NBC companies with 874 vehicles (in 1982) and a huge operating area, which extended all the way from Manchester and Liverpool through the North West up to the Borders. It had a reputation for a high-quality paint finish on its vehicles. Leyland Leopard/Weymann DP49F looks superb in its NBC local coach livery. This vehicle is preserved in its original livery.

Southdown 730 (SCD 730N), Hove Conway Street Garage

Stood outside the large Southdown garage in Conway Street, Hove, which was the former Brighton, Hove & District garage, 730 (SCD 730N) was a Leyland Atlantean with Park Royal bodywork. Similar vehicles were operated by London Country, Ribble, Northern General group, East Yorkshire and Yorkshire Woollen. Both in single- and dual-door versions were available. Delivered in a batch of forty-seven vehicles, the final six were finished by Roe, though they looked identical to the Park Royal buses.

Southdown 627 (UFG 627S), North Street, Brighton, November 1985

Brighton, Hove & District had been taken over by Southdown in 1969. Some vehicles involved carried NBC corporate 'Southdown BH&D' lettering, though it was discontinued in 1974. In the early 1980s Southdown was selected to be broken up ready for deregulation, so in 1984 vehicles started to carry local prefixes to the fleet name such as 'Mid & East Sussex' and 'Brighton & Hove'. The latter also adopted the original red and cream colour that the fleet had carried before 1972. In the end only the Brighton & Hove operation would be sold as a separate fleet from Southdown. 627 (UFG 627S) was a Bristol VRT new in 1977 with dual-door ECW bodywork.

Southdown Portsmouth (Hilsea) Garage, June 1977

Southdown had garages on both sides of London Road, Hilsea, with the largest allocation in the fleet of 100 vehicles. The larger building can be seen on the opposite side of the road to a number of East Kent and local Southdown vehicles awaiting use on the occasion of the Queen Silver Jubilee Naval Fleet Review in June 1977, a time when a number of extra buses were brought in from other NBC companies to help move visitors.

Southdown Portsmouth (Hilsea) Garage, April 1985

Southdown's other garage building on London Road, Hilsea, was on the westerly side of the road, oddly behind a filling station. Both Hilsea garage buildings survived into privatisation, but, like many NBC garages, were prized for their redevelopment value. Of the two only this garage survives in use today with First Solent.

Southdown Bognor Garage, 14 April 1977

A line up of classic Southdown Northern Counties double-deckers are seen outside Bognor garage in April 1977. Leyland PD3 315 and Leyland Titans 405/349 are all full-fronted half cabs, known as Queen Marys, popular with Southdown (Ribble also had similar buses). The other bus was 383, a Daimler Fleetline with a traditional front-entrance body.

Southdown 620 (UWV 620S), Eastbourne Marine Parade

Southdown's operating area covered a number of resort towns, and the company provided open-top buses to cover summer sightseeing tours. Seen on the seafront in Eastbourne, Bristol VRT 620 departs for nearby Beachy Head.

Southdown 1292 (VCD 292S), Clarence Pier, Southsea, 1986

Southdown 1292 started use with the company in 1978 in NBC coach white livery. It was later painted in yellow/black Venetian blind livery. By 1986 the livery had been modified with additional green on the lower sides and the large Southdown name had been replaced with 'South Coast Express' vinyls. 1292 was allocated to Worthing garage when seen here in front of Southsea pier.

Southern Vectis 690 (RDL 690X), Ryde Garage Yard, June 1984

Looking superb in the sunshine outside Ryde garage, Leyland Olympians 690 (RDL 690X), new in April 1982, and 692 (WDL 692Y), parked alongside, would have been some of the last buses the company ordered before deregulation. 690 was the first bus painted in the new green/sand livery the company adopted post-1986.

Southern Vectis 305 (EDL 267V), Shanklin Garage

305 (EDL 267V) is seen outside the company's Shanklin garage. A Willowbrook 003-bodied Bedford YMT, it later gained 'Wightrider' similar to 418 seen overleaf. The company operated six garages across the island, with its workshops and head office located in Newport.

Southern Vectis 121 (YDL 942L)

Uniquely amongst NBC constituents, Southern Vectis was allowed to retain Fountain Coaches livery of orange/cream (which was the same livery as pre-nationalised Shamrock & Rambler on the mainland), devoid of any NBC logos and using a non-standard typeface for the fleet name. The Bedford chassis found favour with Southern Vectis coaches and 121 (YDL 842L) was a Bedford YRT with a Duple C53F body.

Southern Vectis Ryde Garage Yard, mid-1980s

A typical selection of Southern Vectis types can be seen in this 1980s view. New in 1981, Leyland Atlantean 690 (RDL 690X), Bedford YMT 418 (ODL 175R) in 'Wightrider' livery, 304 (XDL 304T), another Bedford YMT, several Leyland Nationals, Bristol REs and the Bristol FS training vehicle in yellow. Note the use of DL registration – at this time the island still issued its own two-letter codes.

Southern Vectis 410 (SDL 743J)

Though Southern Vectis had a typical BTC service bus fleet of Bristol/ECWs, its coach fleet was more eclectic. Southern Vectis was unusual in the NBC for operating twin steer coaches as they suited the island roads, a type more often found with independent operators (Hants & Dorset also operated a small number). 410 (SDL 743J) was a Bedford VAL70 with a Plaxton body.

South Wales 649 (DCY 411K), Quadrant Bus Station, 1981

South Wales had fifty Bristol REs with both ECW and Marshall bodywork. The majority were ordered by or were ex-Western Welsh. 649 (DCY 411K) was in the last three, which were the only ones ordered by SWT. It is seen here entering the then new Quadrant bus station, which was built with the city's new indoor shopping centre and is still in use today.

South Wales 288 (FCY 288W), Gorseinon Bus Station

South Wales bought a number of lightweight buses. In 1980/81 another batch of Bedfords (YMQ) was bought with Duple Dominant bus bodywork (280–297), a body type already fitted to the Ford R1014s purchased in 1976. The first seven were fitted with dual-purpose seating (280–287), see 283 on the next page, and painted in NBC local coach livery. The remainder were fitted with bus seats. 288 is seen loading in Gorseinon, with a journey of 6 miles to reach its destination.

South Wales 225 (PWN 225M), Haverfordwest Bus Station

An unusual purchase for an NBC constituent, South Wales bought two batches of Bedford YRT/YTQ with Willowbrook Express coach bodywork in two lengths. 225 was a Bedford YRQ with the shorter C45F bodywork. Nine were new in 1973/74. The longer Bedford YRT batch of four (509–512) had DP51F bodywork, and all were painted in NBC local coach livery, though towards the end of their use a few were painted National coach white. Behind is one of the four Western Welsh Leyland Atlanteans/Northern Counties that came with Haverfordwest garage in 1972, when the far west area of Western Welsh operations was transferred to South Wales Transport or Crosville. In April 1979 these four vehicles rejoined their original batch when they were transferred to National Welsh.

South Wales 283 (FCY 283Y), Haverfordwest Garage, 1983

In 1980/81 the company purchased another batch of Bedfords (YMQ) but with Duple Dominant bus bodywork (280–297), a body type already fitted to the Ford R1014s purchased in 1976. The first seven were fitted with dual-purpose seating (280–287) and painted in NBC local coach livery. In the mid-1980s they received a version of the NBC Venetian blind livery, but with South Wales fleet names in a gold serif typeface. 283 is seen outside its home garage with local 'Cleddau' identity. These buses all found future work with independents across the country after withdrawal.

South Wales Quadrant Bus Station

The old and new order are seen opposite the Quadrant bus station in Swansea. AEC Regent V 861 (WCY 981C) was a 'short' Willowbrook-bodied version, one of twenty-one delivered in 1965. The AEC Regent/ Renown was a common sight on the roads of West Glamorgan, some lasting long enough to receive 'De Cymru' NBC fleet names. Alongside is Bristol RE 642 (ACY 642K) and Bristol VRT 939 (TWN 939S). Parked in the bays are a number of Leyland Nationals, a Ford R1014, a Bristol RE, an AEC Reliance, an AEC Regent and another Bristol VRT.

South Wales 934 (WCY 710), Ravenhill Yard, 28 April 1976

South Wales has a large central workshop and garage at Ravenhill, where ex-United Welsh (341) Bristol Lodekka FS6G 934 turns in the yard. In the background is Leyland Nationals 761/727 and a Marshall-bodied Bristol RE, which all appear to have been recently recovered. The garage at Ravenhill was opened in 1937 and enlarged in 1939 with the addition of the central workshops. After 1985 it would also become the location for the company's head office. United Welsh had its own central works at Neath Abbey, which was retained for a short time after the companies merged.

Midland General 576 (ORB 576P), Heanor, 1977

Leyland Atlantean/ECW 576 (ORB 576P) was one of the last vehicles delivered to Midland General before all vehicles were lettered with Trent fleet names from 1977. In a batch of six vehicles, unfortunately when only a few days old, two were in Derby's Meadow Road garage fire. One was completely lost (573), while 571's (ONN 576P) chassis was saved but required a new body. ECW could not undertake the work, so Willowbrook fitted a new body, creating a unique version in the fleet.

Trent 338 (SJA 353K), Buxton

The Stockport 'JA' registration indicates Bristol RE/Marshall 338 was not an original Trent vehicle. New to North Western, it had been transferred to Trent along with the garages in Buxton and Matlock in 1972. The intake of vehicles from NWRCC were all similar to existing Trent types, unlike neighbouring Crosville, which, in taking NWRCC vehicles, gained many types unfamiliar to its fleet.

Trent 703 (XAU 703Y), Derby Garage

The successor to the Bristol VRT was the Leyland Olympian. Trent's first batch was delivered in 1983, numbered 700–706 (XAU 700–5Y, XCH 707Y). 703 and 704 are seen at Derby's Meadow Road garage in the mid-1980s. All seven would serve with the privatised company in red and silver livery until 1996–98, and several were sold to Blackpool Transport for further use.

Midland General 357 (FRB 209H), Kirkby in Ashfield, April 1973

In 1972 the NBC reorganised its East Midland constituents. Midland General was amalgamated with Derby-based Trent, not Mansfield District, which it had close connections with. Mansfield District was moved to East Midland management, though initially all four retained their own identity. Midland General was even allowed to retain a shade of blue; the NBC blue was not standardised as red and green were. Seen whilst working the F1 service from Kirkby to Mansfield, dual-door Bristol RE 357 (FRB 209H) was new in 1969, in a batch of twenty-one delivered up to 1972, including three formerly with Mansfield District.

Trent Nottingham Garage, 13 July 1985

Housing sixty-five vehicles (in 1982), Trent's Manvers Street garage in Nottingham was located near to the city's own Corporation bus garage. In 1982 Trent operated fifteen garages. Matlock and Buxton were formerly North Western RCC; Alfreton, Ilkeston, and Langley Mill were ex-Midland General (Underwood had closed in 1977); Trent had closed its own garage in Alfreton in 1977; and the Mansfield garage in Chesterfield Road had been jointly operated with East Midland until September 1979.

Midland General 135 (BNN 101C), *c.* 1974

Bristol MW/ECW DP43F 135 was new as Mansfield District 213 in 1965. It passed to Midland General in 1968 and in October 1976 to Trent. Seen on an excursion duty with Midland General fleet names in NBC local coach livery, in 1972 MGOC company painted a number of coaches in cream with a deep blue central band with white corporate lettering, but no vehicles received the blue/white version of NBC local coach livery. 135 would later receive Trent fleet names on this livery.

United Durham Garage, 26 May 1979

United was one of the largest NBC constituents with 883 vehicles (in 1982). Its operating area was vast, stretching from Scarborough and Ripon in the south to the Scottish border with a joint Scottish Bus Group garage in Berwick, along with garages within Northern General's Newcastle area. Durham, with seventy-two vehicles, had the largest allocation in the company. United Automobile located its headquarters and central workshops in Darlington.

United 6073 (SHN 73L)

Looking unusual with a Bristol LH front, 6073 was one of United's large fleet of Bristol REs, delivered in a batch of thirty in 1972/73. It was fitted with ECW forty-nine-seat dual-purpose bodywork. Seen in 1987, it carries Scarborough & District identity. Operations in Scarborough had passed to East Yorkshire in 1986, and the application of these fleet names and the NBC logo was for a brief period only.

United Newcastle Portland Terrace Garage, 7 September 1985

Though the Northern General Group was the main NBC operator on Tyneside, United operated two garages in Newcastle – one at Gallowgate with forty-eight vehicles, which also operated as a coach station, and the one pictured above, at Portland Terrace, with fifty-six vehicles. Built in 1930, it incorporates Greek Doric columns between its six doorways. Unusually, this building remained in its intended use with Arriva until recently.

United Whitley Bay Garage, 6 September 1985

Located with the bus station, Whitley Bay garage was just off the Promenade. With an allocation of twenty-eight vehicles, by 1985 many were painted in the Tyne & Wear PTE livery for service within the PTE zone. Note the ex-Thames Valley Bristol LH, which was converted by United to a Uniform store (63). It later became a staff mess room.

United Counties 227 (MRP 227P), Bournemouth, 21 August 1977

United Counties 227, a Leyland Leopard with Alexander T type coach bodywork, stands in the National Travel South West parking ground in Bournemouth, using the benefit of being part of the National Bus Company. The Alexander T type was unusual south of the border. United Counties purchased five in 1976 and all were painted in Central Activities white livery. (D. Mant)

United Counties 157 (157 BRP), Wellingborough Garage, 14 May 1978

United Counties Bristol MW 157 (157 BRP) is seen withdrawn in the yard of Wellingborough garage in 1978. The additional chrome indicates this bus had originally been a dual-purpose vehicle. In 1974 it was fitted with bus seats and repainted from dual-purpose livery. It was withdrawn in March 1978. Behind is Bristol MW 144 (WBD 144), another former DP41F vehicle, which was withdrawn slightly earlier in December 1977. Just visible is AEC Matador recovery 97(20), which had been withdrawn in 1975. (D. Mant)

United Counties 1018 (620 LFM), Bedford Garage, 14 May 1978

United Counties purchased a number of Bristol LDs from other NBC fleets in 1973. The Cheshire 'FM' registration indicates this vehicle had come from Crosville. Numbered DLG10 in the Crosville fleet, it was used for three years by its new owner as bus 576 before United Counties converted it to replace its Bristol K5G tree-lopper. Numbered 1018 in its service fleet, the conversion in October 1975 involved removing a section of the roof and fitting a fold-out platform on the upper deck, which was on the opposite side to the photo. Withdrawn in September 1980, it was in turn replaced by Bristol FS 1004 (KBD 713D), which was ready in January 1981. (D. Mant)

United Counties 194 (GRP 922N), Bedford Garage, 14 May 1978

To ease the company's vehicle issues, between 1973 and 1976 United Counties bought twenty-five Bedford YRTs and thirty-four of the shorter Bedford YRQ, both with Willowbrook 001 lightweight bodies, an unusual choice for an NBC constituent. South Wales had similar with both Bedford and Ford chassis and United and Maidstone & District had second-hand examples. (D. Mant)

United Counties 072 (PKX 272R), Leighton Buzzard, August 1976

United Counties operated a number of minibuses long before other NBC constituents adopted widespread use. The company purchased a variety of designs including a twelve-seater Ford Transit used for community services in Northamptonshire and fifteen-seat Mercedes/Deansgate for Milton Keynes dial-a-ride. 072 (PKX 272R) was one of two Ford A series fitted with Tricentrol bodies, operated in conjunction with Bedfordshire County Council for Leighton Buzzard town services from 1976. The NBC had directed the use of local coach livery for minibuses, irrespective of the seating type. The Fords were replaced on these services by Bedford YMQs/Lex (shortened by Tricentrol) in May 1981.

United Counties 1003 t/p 596BD (URP 999), Bedford Garage, 14 May 1978

United Counties 1003 was an ex-Army Foden DG6/10 lorry bought by the company in July 1956. Originally numbered 99, it had come via British Road Service. Converted using Bristol MW parts, it was allocated to Bedford garage. It was withdrawn in October 1978 when it was replaced by Ford D800 Recovery 1037 (DGP 363H), which had been rebuilt by the company using a long wheelbase Ford D chassis. (D. Mant)

West Riding Selby Garage, 23 September 1984

West Riding's smallest garage (twenty-two vehicles in 1982) was at Selby. It was also the company's most easterly garage. The company had depots at Castleford, Wakefield (Belle Isle and Savile Street) and Featherstone.

Yorkshire Woollen Dewsbury Garage, 4 June 1975

Yorkshire Woollen in the NBC had garages at Dewbury and Heckmondwike. The West Riding Group had a large number of Daimler Fleetlines with bodywork from several builders. The six Yorkshire Woollens seen here all had Alexander H41/31F bodies. From left to right 605, 592, 594, 591, 597 and 602 are seen in Dewsbury yard.

Yorkshire Woollen 159 (SCP 562), Dewsbury Garage, 1973

The NBC joined the fleets of West Riding Automobile and Yorkshire Woollen District Transport to become the West Riding Group in the early 1970s. The joint name was carried on dual-purpose and service vehicles, but buses retained a single fleet name. 159 (SCP 562) was a 1963 Leyland Leopard with Willowbrook B53F bodywork. It was previously Hebble 682.

Yorkshire Woollen 193 (BHD 208C), Dewsbury, 28 December 1975

193 (BHD 208C) stands at Dewsbury garage in 1975. Only the 'YORKSHIRE' fleet name was applied to Woollen District buses, with the transfers often applied to the front and rear as well. 193 was a 1965 Leyland Leopard with Marshall B53F bodywork.

West Riding 232 (LHL 176F), Castleford Bus Station, March 1976

West Riding was still an independent bus company before it was sold to THC in 1967. The fleet was therefore unlike surrounding nationalised companies and some of this independent influence lasted into the NBC era. 232 (LHL 176F) was a Leyland Panther with Marshall B51F bodywork, a type more usually found in municipal or PTE fleets.

West Riding 281 (PHL 240G), Midland Street, Barnsley, March 1978

Another Leyland Panther, though fitted with a Plaxton Derwent B52F body, an uncommon body type in the NBC. 281 (PHL 240G) is seen passing the Yorkshire Traction Travel Centre with the remains of the Midland Railways route through the town above in Midland Street, Barnsley, soon after leaving the town's bus station. West Riding had carried a dark green livery before 1972. Interestingly, poppy red was chosen (Yorkshire Woolen was red) for the amalgamated fleets. Bristol RE 308 (UHL 941J) was the only West Riding vehicle to receive corporate lettering on a green livery.

West Riding 166 (BJX 132C), Dewsbury Paint Shop, May 1973

Before the joint Yorkshire/West Riding fleet names were applied to the company's dual-purpose vehicles, newly repainted 166 (BJX 132C), an AEC Reliance/Park Royal DP39F, awaits re-entry to service. This vehicle was new to Hebble (132) in a batch of four in 1965. By 1974 it had received West Riding fleet names. Hebble lost its bus services in 1972, being transferred to Yorkshire Woollen, West Riding and Halifax/Calderdale JOC, though the Hebble name was retained for a time on National white coaches. Oddly, of the four only three passed to the NBC; the other (BJX 134C) went to Calderdale JOC, lasting into WYPTE ownership. 166 would find further use with Caelloi Motors in North Wales.

West Riding/Yorkshire 65 (AHL 727K), Wakefield Bus Station

West Riding 65 (AHL 727K) was a Leyland Leopard with dual-purpose Plaxton bodywork, formerly numbered 327 and new in 1971 in a batch of five. In the mid-1970s, the group's dual-purpose vehicles carried both fleet names in a small-sized font, as seen on 65, leaving Wakefield bus station for Newstead.

West Riding 8 (HWY 724N), Wakefield Bus Station, 1985

Before the Duple/Plaxton grant coaches arrived in the mid-1970s, West Riding used a mix of Alexander Y types, Plaxton 'Derwents' and a few former standard-bodied BETs from Yorkshire Woollen for its local coach fleet. Lightly loaded 8 (HWY 724N) departs from Wakefield bus station for Pontefract. It was formerly numbered 384, in a batch of eleven (378–388) new in 1975. By this time Alexander had revised the front grille.

Yorkshire Woollen 506 (HD 8562), Dewsbury Garage, 1973

Yorkshire Woollen 506 (HD 8562) was a Leyland PS2/5 'Tiger', delivered as a single-deck bus. The chassis was new as long ago as 1950, though it was rebodied by Roe in 1963. In a batch of five (502–507), they would be withdrawn in the mid-1970s, some lasting long enough to receive NBC poppy red livery.

West Riding 667 (PHL 232G), Leeds Bus Station, July 1981

West Riding/Yorkshire Woollen operated a large fleet of Daimler Fleetlines, fitted with bodies from Alexander, Northern Counties, Roe and ECW. 667 (PHL 232G) was fitted with the Roe version, new in 1969. Based in Leeds, the Roe bodywork was a popular choice in South and West Yorkshire, with both PTEs using the company. Its use by the NBC was far more unusual.

West Riding Castleford Garage, 23 September 1984

Castleford had the second largest allocation in the West Riding Group with eighty-three vehicles. Only Wakefield's Belle Isle garage with 136 vehicles was larger. The three buses visible outside the garage in September 1984 had all received the joint West Yorkshire PTE 'Metrobus' lettering applied to the company's vehicles operating from a garage within the PTE zone. Just visible is West Riding Leyland Tiger/Alexander TE 28 (EWY 28Y). The company had very few National white coaches. These carried the NBC Venetian blind on white livery.

West Yorkshire 1217 (HWW 479C), Harrogate Bus Station, July 1975

West Yorkshire was a typical Tilling company fleet. The majority of the vehicles were of Bristol/ECW origin. Operating over 200 Bristol REs, including a number of the earliest ones, which featured the unusual curved front, 1217 (HWW 479C), new in 1965, illustrates this design feature. Surrounded by Bristol LHs, 1217 awaits departure from Harrogate bus station. The town also contained the headquarters, central workshops and separate bodyshop, as well as a large garage.

West Yorkshire 3433 (NWT 715M), York, *c.* 1977

West Yorkshire had an interesting agreement with two of its operating areas, Keighley and York. The company operated joint services with the respective councils. The Keighley arrangement ended in 1973. In York it lasted until 1985. One peculiarity was the retention of Tilling-style gold fleet names, as seen on Leyland National 3422 (NWT 715M). Vehicles in the York fleet used a 3 for the first figure of the fleet number. In April 1981 the use of 'York' in NBC style and the city crest was introduced.

West Yorkshire 2514 (YYG 217G), Scarborough Coach Park

In 1977/78 seven West Yorkshire Bristol RE coaches were rebuilt by Willowbrook with a completely new front styling and one-man operation. The results can be seen on 2514 (ex-1025) (YYG 217G) standing at Scarborough after working the 277 holiday service from Keighley. A controversial rebuilding was not continued after the seven conversions, and all were withdrawn by 1982.

West Yorkshire 2574 (KUB 548V) and 2524 (CWY 503H), East Yorkshire Bridlington Garage

West Yorkshire started to use the 25xx series for dual-purpose vehicles in the late 1970s. Renumbered from CRL6/1036/2306, Bristol RE/ECW coach 2524 had previously been painted in National white livery. A much newer vehicle, 2574 (KUB 548V), a Leyland Leopard/Plaxton Supreme IV, was delivered in NBC local coach livery. The two are seen parked outside the East Yorkshire Bridlington garage whilst working on excursions.

West Yorkshire 1758 (282 BWU), Derby Bus Station

In July 1976 Trent's garage in Meadow Road, Derby, suffered a serious fire; fifty vehicles were damaged or destroyed. The company put out a request to neighbouring NBC companies and Municipal Transport departments. West Yorkshire provided Bristol Lodekkas and new Bristol VRTs. 1758 (282 BWU), a Bristol FS6B new in 1963, seen here in Derby bus station, probably caused some confusion for the local passengers.

West Yorkshire Harrogate Garage, 25 May 1980

West Yorkshire's headquarters and main workshops were located in Harrogate, which was also home to a large garage with an allocation of eighty-two. Outside in May 1980 were Leyland National 1416 (NWT 704M), Bristol RE 1382 (UWX 368L) and a dual-purpose Leyland Leopard.

Western National 1701 (OTT 55), Salisbury Coach Park, 1982

Western National was the last NBC operator using the Bristol LS in passenger service. 1701 was new in 1954 and had the honour of being the last of its type in NBC PSV use. It finished its service at Weymouth garage in 1982, and was seen in Salisbury whilst on a Dorset Transport Circle special. It survives preserved in Southern National livery.

Western National 2915 (619 DDV), Weymouth Garage, 1973

Western National's bus station and garage were located across the road from the town's railway station. It had a second entrance onto the Weymouth Tramway, with one of the company's largest allocations (seventy-three vehicles). In 1973 Bristol 2915 (619 DDV), a Bristol MW/ECW, was still in pre-1972 livery but with white NBC fleet names. Later it received NBC green bus livery, but withdrawal came in 1980. This garage remains in use today with First Group.

Western National Bridport, 20 June 1983

Western National/Devon General had a vast operating area, from Weymouth and Bridgewater all the way to Land's End, covering all of Cornwall and Devon and large parts of Somerset and Dorset. A Bristol LH and LHS with Marshall bodies stand in the open bus station next to the Western National's small garage in Bridport. With a single building, it had an allocation of twenty-two (in 1982). It too survives in First Group use.

Western National (Royal Blue) 1331 (PUO 331M), Bridport

Western National used the Royal Blue fleet names for its National white coaches. 1331 (PUO 331M), a Bristol LH fitted with a Plaxton body, new in 1974, works a National Express service along the coast to Bournemouth. Bridport served as a rest stop for a number of National services, and there was a large parking area for such use. To the right is a locally allocated Bristol LH with unusual Marshall bodywork – 1321 (NTT 321M). These were painted in National white when new and lettered for Royal Blue. Western National downgraded these straight to bus livery, though the coach seats were retained.

Western National 1222 (272 KTA), Totnes Garage, April 1979

Western National was the largest user of the Bristol SU type, operating both SUS (short) and SULs in both bus and coach specification. 1222 (272 KTA) was in the coach specification but had received local coach livery in the NBC era, though a number of these also were painted in NBC bus livery. 1222 was new in July 1962 to Totnes garage where it remained until withdrawal in November 1979. It found further PSV use in the Channel Islands.

Western National 1237 (890 ADV), St Austell Garage, September 1977

Another final survivor with Western National in the NBC was 1237 (890 ADV), an AEC Reliance with Willowbrook Viking body. It was new to Grey Cars in 1959 and was retained by the NBC until 1979, even receiving NBC local coach livery. Allocated to St Austell, it suited the narrow lanes in Cornwall. In 1980 it entered preservation restored in original Grey Cars livery.

Devon General 580 (VOD 590S), Exeter Garage

Devon General vehicles were painted in poppy red from 1972, but in the early 1980s leaf green was adopted like the parent company Western National. Bristol VRT/ECW 580 (VOD 590S) was new to Devon General in 1978 in poppy red. It was sold to South Midland as 648 in February 1988.

Devon General 253 (UFJ 293), Torquay Garage, 21 May 1978

Exeter Corporation had passed to Devon General in April 1970. Former Exeter Corporation Guy Arab/Massey 253 (UFJ 293) is seen with its newly applied poppy red, the only one of the batch to receive NBC livery. Alongside is Guy Arab/Park Royal 256 still in City of Exeter livery. 253 had served in Exeter livery with Devon General NBC fleet names. It would be withdrawn in 1979 after a period of being used as a driver trainer.

Western National Totnes Garage, June 1981

A glimpse into Totnes garage in 1981 shows Bristol LH/ECW 1578 (VOD 109K); Bristol LH/Plaxton 1333 (JFJ 498N), which was ex-National South West in 1978; and Bristol LHS/ECW 1560 (FDV 790V). 1333 had been downgraded to local coach livery with Western National. Most Western National white coaches carried Royal Blue fleet names but the use of Western National and Devon General fleet names was not unknown.

Western National Laira Central Workshops

The Western National Central Workshops were located in Laira, Plymouth, a location that also served as a large garage as well (seventy-nine vehicles). Parked outside was two Leyland Nationals, a Plaxton-bodied Bristol LH, a Bristol FS Trainer and a Marshall-bodied Bristol LH. The company had introduced Cornwall Busways in 1983, when the company was split. The company also had workshops in Exeter and Torquay.

Red & White DS1059 (UWO 710), Brynmawr, July 1974

The Western Welsh group was formed of Western Welsh, Red & White, Rhondda and Jones, all of which carried NBC fleet names for various periods. Red & White operated across the English border into the Forest of Dean in Gloucestershire. Western Welsh had started with a large operating area but lost all its west Wales services to South Wales and Crosville in 1972. The fleet was interesting with the two large companies having different vehicle types from their BET and Tillings origins. Red & White was a typical Bristol/ECW fleet. DS1059 (UWO 710), a Bristol MW with an ECW coach body, by 1973 was in the dual-purpose role. It was renumbered UD1059 in August 1974 and withdrawn soon after in 1975.

Red & White UD663

Another downgraded Bristol MW, Red & White UC663 (28 FAX) was new in 1962, with revised ECW bodywork. Renumbered in October 1975 to UC6163, interestingly it only carries an NBC logo on the front grille (R&W keenly applied the double N logo to the front of vehicles). The fleet name lettering was applied in a non-standard position. It was sold in 1976.

Rhondda UD3372 (XBO 529K)

The NBC allowed the retention of the Rhondda fleet name for vehicles at Porth garage until the formation of National Welsh in 1978. Only a handful of dual-purpose vehicles received the fleet name on local coach livery. This Leyland Leopard with DP47F Marshall body was Western Welsh 1529, then UD972, becoming UD3372 in October 1975. It had carried Western Welsh NBC identity and later National Welsh in 1978.

Jones UD1174 (GHB 682N), Newport Bus Station

UD1174 was new to Jones in 1975 in their NBC blue livery, which they would retain until January 1981 – three years after the three other companies had become National Welsh. Though Jones was the smallest NBC constituent fleet, it had a fascinating mix of vehicles including types found in both Western Welsh and Red & White fleets.

Jones UD1668 (OWO 755F), Jones Garage Aberbeeg

Jones operated a full fleet including buses and dual-purpose and white National coaches with Jones fleet names in blue, but only using single-deck vehicles. UD1668 passes the company's only garage. It was a Willowbrook-bodied Leyland Leopard that was new in April 1968 (21). It would last long enough to receive National Welsh lettering as U3568. Note the lack of route number.

Red & White Monmouth Garage

Though both fleet names are carried on the building, Monmouth was originally a Red & White garage. Seen here are three Red & White Bristol MWs and the locally allocated Bedford RL recovery lorry E26 (YWO 342H) on trade plates 009 AX, which was withdrawn in 1981.

Red & White Brynmawr Garage, c. 1974

A selection of Bristol/ECW products including a rare Bristol Lodekka FL. L1960 (19 AAX) with its long body was one of sixteen Red & Whites taken delivery of in 1960. The Red & White numbering scheme included a prefix letter to indicate vehicle type and the figure included the vehicle number and years of purchase. This was an L type, the nineteenth vehicle new in 1960. Western Welsh adopted this system when the fleets were amalgamated.

Red & White Bulwark Garage, *c.* 1974

Red & White located its central workshops in Bulwark, just outside Chepstow. There was also a running garage on the same site. A couple of Bristol Lodekkas and the refueling point are visible in this view. The central workshops were a much bigger site located behind the photographer. Western Welsh had its own central works in Ely, Cardiff, but work was concentrated here when the Ely site was closed in the 1970s.

Rhonnda UD4168 (UTG 320F), Bulwark Workshops, Chepstow

Seen in the yard of the Western Welsh Group central workshops at Bulwark in the mid-1970s, Rhondda UD4168's fleet number indicates it is the forty-first underfloor engine dual-purpose vehicle delivered in 1968. The Rhondda fleet name was retained by Western Welsh until the formation of National Welsh.

Red & White Galligaer Street Garage, Cardiff

Both Red & White and Western Welsh had garages in Cardiff. Red & White's was in Gelligaer Street, while Western Welsh had premises at Penarth Road, Cowbridge Road West and the Ely workshops. Gelligaer Street became the main coaching garage for Red & White and was still in use when National Welsh was formed. It was closed in March 1986.

Red & White Abergavenny Garage

Interestingly, views of NBC garages can be hard to find. Often fascinating locations, in the 1970s permission to look inside was usually granted or could be obtained in advance from company headquarters in the form of a permit. Red & White proudly pronounce their ownership on the building. This, along with the rest of the company's operational premises, would become National Welsh in 1981.

National Welsh MD1377 (SKG 892S)

Western Welsh purchased eight Leyland EA/Asco Clubman DP19F minibuses in 1977/78: MD1177–1477 and MD1178–1478 (DP20F). Delivered in NBC poppy red, some including MD1977 were later painted in green/ yellow 'Village Bus' livery for dedicated services around Cowbridge. Vehicles for these services were replaced by narrow-bodied Bristol LHSs in 1981/82. The eight vehicles were allocated to garages including Bridgend and Cwmbran. Two of these Leyland EAs were transferred to service use. MD1377 became publicity vehicle E25 in December 1981, but was finally withdrawn in March 1983.

Red & White R 2567 (LAX 123F), Cinderford Garage, 22 June 1977

Like Crosville, Red & White straddled the border of England and Wales. Its English operating area was contracted in the 1960s, but it retained areas around the Forest of Dean including Cinderford, Gloucestershire, where Bristol RE R2567 was new in 1967 with ECW DP50F bodywork. The coach seats were still fitted. Downgraded to a bus, it was seen outside the Red & White garage in Cinderford, which, like Monmouth seen earlier, by 1977 carried both company's fleet names.

National Welsh Porth Garage Yard

An interesting selection of typical National Welsh vehicles in the yard of the former Rhondda garage at Porth. A number had been withdrawn from service. By this time the Rhondda fleet names had been discontinued. The roof of the large garage building can be seen in the background. The National Welsh fleet, being formed from Red & White, Western Welsh, Rhondda and Jones, had a fascinating fleet from the mixed former BTC/BET fleets.

National Welsh E29 t/p 331 AX, Bulwark Central Workshops

Bristol MW, towing bus E29, is seen inside the Bulwark central workshops. It was converted in April 1979 from bus U4362 (18 FAX). It was allocated to Aberdare garage, becoming E1060 in the 1983 renumbering scheme. It was sold in August 1985 to dealer Martin in Middlewich.

Yorkshire Traction Barnsley Garage, 10 August 1985

Yorkshire Traction, or 'Tracky' as it was known locally, had a fleet of 340 in 1982 and operated six garages. Its central workshops were located with its Barnsley garage in Upper Sheffield Road. The location contained a number of buildings. The one seen here has the company's Magirus heavy recovery vehicle visible inside the entrance. Note Lincolnshire Bristol VRT 1916 (JTL 771N), which had just been repainted by Yorkshire Traction, not an unusual occurrence when the NBC existed, where companies could work for other constituents.

Yorkshire Traction 232 (UHE 232H), Barnsley Garage, February 1974

The Alexander Y type was a popular choice with South/West Yorkshire bus operators, both NBC and PTE. Yorkshire Traction operated this type in both NBC dual-purpose and bus livery, getting its maximum use out of these vehicles. YTC 232 was renumbered 132 in December 1979 and received a later-style front grille molding and deeper application of the white upper paint. It was withdrawn in 1981. Yorkshire Traction had a mix of Leyland Leopards with Alexander- and BET-style bodies for the majority of its dual-purpose fleet before Grant coaches were purchased for these duties. The NBC developed its 'White Rose' express network throughout West and South Yorkshire and the NBC constituent company's local coach vehicles were a common sight across the conurbation.

Yorkshire Traction 234 (LWE 234W), Pontefract Bus Station

Leyland National 2 234 (LWE 234W) waits in Pontefract bus station with the 245 service to Barnsley Interchange. The bus station in Barnsley was located between the town's two railway stations, though only one remained open in the 1970s. New in April 1981, 234 spent its entire life with Yorkshire Traction, being scrapped by the privatised company in 2004. The company also operated two Leyland National 2 (262/3) with coach seating in green and white 'X20 Fastline' livery for its limited stop service between Doncaster and Barnsley in 1982.

Yorkshire Traction 752 (XHE 752J), Midland Street, Barnsley, March 1978

Seen in Midland Street, Barnsley, just down from West Riding, is 281 (PHL 240G), illustrated earlier. Though Yorkshire Traction 752 (XHE 752J) is on home territory, Yorkshire Traction had its offices, central workshops and a large garage in Barnsley. 752 (XHE 752J), a Daimler Fleetline/Park Royal, was in a batch of five that had been ordered by Sheffield Joint Omnibus Committee, but delivered to YTC.

National Samuelsons ULW 486M, February 1974

The Central Activities Group initially contained numerous fleet names and is a fascinating subject in its own right. Interest was never as much as it was was in the individual bus companies, though NT South West produced an illustrated fleet list, and Ribble included details of Standerwick in its official fleet list. One of the more unusual vehicles was Samuelson ULW 486M, a Ford Transit with Stratchen B12F body. It was purchased in August 1973 specifically to operate a shuttle between Victoria Railway and Coach Station, for a 6p fare! It was transferred to National Travel South East, then in 1976 to NT (Midlands). Seen inside Samuelson's Victoria garage, the company's Bedford RL recovery (t/p 627LA) vehicle is visible parked behind.

Greenslades 288 (AFJ 82B)

Greenslades had been previously associated with Devon General. With the formation of the NBC it was moved into one of the five regional National travel companies – National (South West), Black & White, Shamrock & Rambler and Wessex, though most of the early Central Activities Group fleet names were phased out for simply National South West. Greenslades 288 (AFJ 82B) was an AEC Reliance with Harrington Cavalier bodywork built to a narrow specification for the company. The name Greenslades was reintroduced in 1983 for Devon General coaches.